PRIMATES

SPIDER MONKEYS

BY TRUDY BECKER

WWW.APEXEDITIONS.COM

Apex is distributed by North Star Editions:
sales@northstareditions.com | 888-417-0195

Produced for Apex by Red Line Editorial.

Photographs ©: iStockphoto, cover, 6; Shutterstock Images, 1, 10–11, 12, 13, 14, 16–17, 18–19, 22–23, 24, 26–27, 29; Ignacio Palacios/Photodisc/Getty Images, 4–5; Bill Gozansky/Alamy, 8–9; Carol Farneti-Foster/Photodisc/Getty Images, 20; Mara & Moritz Wolf/ImageBroker/Getty Images, 21

Library of Congress Control Number: 2025939160

ISBN
979-8-89250-799-8 (hardcover)
979-8-89250-828-5 (paperback)
979-8-89250-884-1 (ebook pdf)
979-8-89250-857-5 (hosted ebook)

Printed in the United States of America
Mankato, MN
012026

NOTE TO PARENTS AND EDUCATORS

Apex books are designed to build literacy skills in striving readers. Exciting, high-interest content attracts and holds readers' attention. The text is carefully leveled to allow students to achieve success quickly. Additional features, such as bolded glossary words for difficult terms, help build comprehension.

TABLE OF CONTENTS

CHAPTER 1

YELL, SHAKE, AND THROW

It is a warm day in the Brazilian rainforest. A group of white-cheeked spider monkeys sits high in the branches. Below them, a jaguar creeps closer.

Spider monkeys stay safe from attackers by living high up in trees.

One spider monkey spots the jaguar. The monkey barks loudly. Other spider monkeys join in. Then they shake the tree branches to scare the jaguar.

NOISY MONKEYS

Spider monkeys make many different noises. They often bark at **intruders**. They whinny like horses to find one another. The monkeys also **communicate** with squeaks and whoops.

Jaguars can climb trees to hunt.

A spider monkey's call can be heard from more than 1.2 miles (2 km) away.

FAST FACT

Spider monkeys' main **predators** are snakes, large birds, and big cats.

The jaguar keeps coming closer. So, the monkeys break off small branches. They throw the sticks down at the jaguar. Finally, it slinks away. The monkeys are safe.

CHAPTER 2

ALL ABOUT SPIDER MONKEYS

Spider monkeys are small **primates**. There are seven **species** of spider monkeys. Most weigh between 12 and 20 pounds (5 and 9 kg). Some can grow about 2 feet (61 cm) tall.

Guiana spider monkeys are the largest species of spider monkeys.

Spider monkeys have long, strong tails. They use their tails to hang and swing on branches. They can even pick things up with their tails.

FAST FACT
Spider monkeys are the only primates without thumbs. They use their tails to grab things instead.
Spider monkeys can hold on to branches with just their tails.

Spider monkeys live in Central and South America. The monkeys mostly stay in **tropical** rainforests. They may also live in other wooded areas.

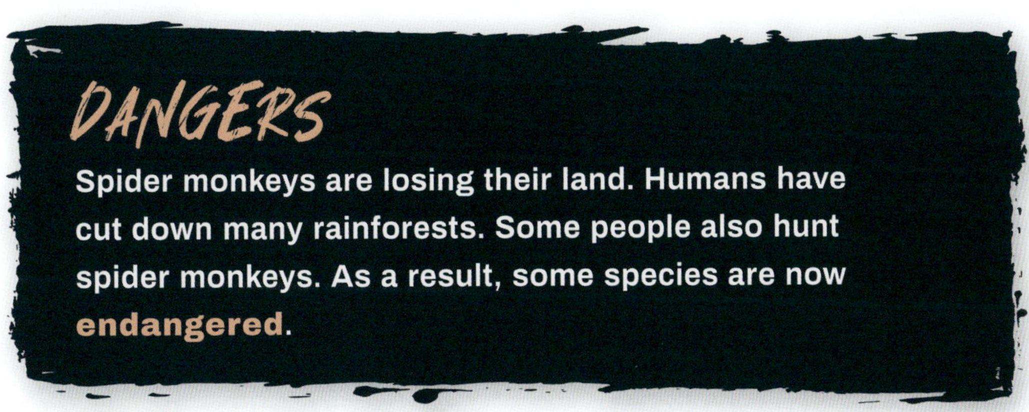

DANGERS

Spider monkeys are losing their land. Humans have cut down many rainforests. Some people also hunt spider monkeys. As a result, some species are now **endangered**.

◀ Many spider monkeys live in the Amazon Rainforest.

CHAPTER 3

Spider monkeys eat mostly fruit. They also eat nuts and seeds. Sometimes they even catch spiders and insects.

Fruit makes up about 80 percent of what a spider monkey eats.

Some spider monkeys can leap 30 feet (9 m) between trees.

Spider monkeys rarely go down to the ground. They spend their days searching for food in the forest's canopy. They sleep up high, too.

In some species, female spider monkeys lead the groups.

Spider monkeys are social animals. They live in groups called troops. Troops often have up to 40 members. But some have up to 100 members.

USING TOOLS

Spider monkeys use sticks to scratch themselves. They also rub squished leaves on their bodies. That may help keep insects away.

Troops may break into smaller groups when looking for food.

CHAPTER 4

LIFE CYCLE

Spider monkeys can **mate** throughout the year. Each female gives birth about seven months after mating. She has one baby at a time.

A female spider monkey has a baby about every two to four years.

For the first year, babies depend on their mothers. Each mother feeds her baby and keeps it safe. She also teaches it to communicate and find food.

HANGING ON

For four months, a baby spider monkey clings to its mother's stomach. After that, the baby rides on her back. It uses its tail to hold on. The baby's tail wraps around its mother's tail.

◀ **When spider monkeys are about 18 months old, they start looking for food on their own.**

Spider monkeys are fully grown when they are four or five years old. At that time, some monkeys leave. They find new troops. Others stay with their home troops.

FAST FACT

Spider monkeys live for about 22 years in the wild.

Female spider monkeys are more likely to leave their home troops than males are.

COMPREHENSION QUESTIONS

Write your answers on a separate piece of paper.

1. Write a few sentences describing the main ideas of Chapter 4.

2. Do you think having a tail like a spider monkey's would be useful? Why or why not?

3. How many species of spider monkeys are there?

- **A.** 7
- **B.** 22
- **C.** 40

4. Why might spider monkeys use different sounds to communicate?

- **A.** because each sound means something different
- **B.** because other monkeys don't know what the sounds mean
- **C.** so that the sounds will be harder to hear

5. What does **canopy** mean in this book?

*Spider monkeys rarely go down to the ground. They spend their days searching for food in the forest's **canopy**.*

A. the forest floor
B. an area high in the trees
C. a spot by the water

6. What does **social** mean in this book?

*Spider monkeys are **social** animals. They live in groups called troops.*

A. likely to spend time with others
B. likely to spend time alone
C. likely to be a predator

Answer key on page 32.

GLOSSARY

communicate

To send and receive messages.

endangered

In danger of dying out forever.

intruders

Animals that go into areas where they are not welcome.

mate

To form a pair and come together to have babies.

predators

Animals that hunt and eat other animals.

primates

Animals in a group that includes apes and monkeys.

species

Groups of animals or plants that are similar and can breed with one another.

tropical

Having weather that is often warm and wet.

unique

Different from all others.

BOOKS

McCarthy, Cecilia Pinto. *Rain Forest Biomes*. Abdo Publishing, 2024.

Murray, Julie. *Fun Facts About Monkeys*. Abdo Publishing, 2022.

Schuh, Mari. *Animals of the Amazon Rain Forest*. Capstone Publishing, 2022.

ONLINE RESOURCES

Visit **www.apexeditions.com** to find links and resources related to this title.

ABOUT THE AUTHOR

Trudy Becker lives in Minneapolis, Minnesota. She likes exploring new places and loves anything involving books.

INDEX

ANSWER KEY:

1. Answers will vary; 2. Answers will vary; 3. A; 4. A; 5. B; 6. A